Hopeless Heart: Poetry

Love, Loss, and Light in the Dark

Madeline Blue

i

Find Madeline's poetry and songs in progress @littleladyditties on Instagram and a portfolio of her other written works at www.madeline.blue.

DEDICATION

To Dad, who loves me no matter what.
To Mom, who loved me ferociously.

PREFACE

Let's keep this short. Always plenty to say and so little time.
But as the years flew by, and I flew from East to West, I kept
searching for the same *something*.
To what end, we have yet to discover.
Yet in a flash, it'll all be gone.

Here is a small selection of thousands of thoughts and feelings I
forged in the darkness. If your wounded inner child is anything
like mine, these poems are our shadow expression, uncaged. So if
it suits you, tear out these pages! Tape stanzas that speak to you
on a wall or window. Let's continue on a path to eradicate the
shame of being human, together. I hope to make safe our
desperation for the embrace of a love with undying embers.
Even as we fade.

This is now a place for words that scream to see the light.

Stream of Contents...

Earnest East

Projection

I am just a canvas.
So paint me as you will.

I am just an empty glass
So choose a drink, then fill.

I am to your liking.
Or if, perhaps, I'm not

I am just the undrawn lines
You want from dot to dot.

I do not see myself as well
As you can see me there.

Yes, I know my eyes, my face,
my body and its hair...

But I can't see the looking glass
or lens you see me through.

I do not own your spectacles
and do not share your view.

I try to scope myself as others see me from my stand—
But then, I'm just a painter
with an open
empty
hand.

Labyrinth

I try to turn to silent seeking
But every inch, my brain is peeking
'Round each corner, dark or drab
Seeing overwrought slate or empty slab.

Along extremes I live or die
And love will never ask me why
I chase the labyrinth, rodent-like
No pellets waiting down the pike.

How do I stay above the fray?
I know the path to find my heart—
A sacred chest with worthy lock
And latch, but ticking like a clock.

Divergent

I am swimming in ideas—
But not a solution.

I am drowning in messy magnitude
Screaming! Above the water, you can
Only hear "glug glug glug"—
Watch a woman flailing. Feel
Pity, paired with curiosity.

"It *does* seem she should know how to float!"

My vision board looks crazed—the work of
A Mad Hatter wearing too many styles. I
Look good in hats—they crown and frame a
Furrowed forehead and sinister grin, full of
Self-awareness that smells like cockiness
(Yet certainly wreaks of uncertainty: a latent perfume
That won't be washed away. Even by years
Of confidence-boosting activities, and showers of
Validating glances.)

These romances
I have with my Potential
Are everlasting, but I charge into them
Like flings. Swinging between boldness
And terror, retreating to
Hide under pillows, where my
Fragile heart feels
Safe.

The frailty of my inner child
(Thumb-sucking nonsense and all)
Begs for someone's stable form
To buoy me in this. To see me through the
Buckling overload of watery visions,
Flowing toward my sense of eternity, legacy—
Yet, all at once, away. Yearning to join an unstoppable
Tsunami. Rising consistently toward the surface,
Tiny bubbles beg to catch the wave.

First Lesson in Shame

In sixth grade,
We play a staring game.
He is Alec, and he is smart
And when our eyes meet
I read his mind.

His dark face turns rosy around me
when he giggles. And I'm shy, too, but
do not blush around boys, so much as
splash in the pool of fiery friction—
zig-zagging like electric sparks of red—
that gets me lost in my head
dreaming of fierce love-affairs
on hilltops.

In fourth grade, our families
Ran into each other at the Grand Canyon;
In fifth grade, he asked me
To the Fifth Grade Dance.

In sixth grade,
I play an April Fools' prank:
Pretend to be "Mrs. Shabooboo," the sub—
But on the chalkboard (oops!), in Period Two,
Where Alec and I both excel in Math League,
I've gone and written *MY OWN REAL NAME*.

And Alec, sitting and watching
with "the cool boys"
chortles in an unfamiliar way

as that rotten nerd
with his babyface
comes up to the board
and writes "is a loser"
just to the right of
MY OWN REAL NAME.
I enter a bubble, pink around
the edges of my vision, as
another "cool boy" cackles:
Who would date Madi? What a weird girl.

In Period Three, Alec
guffaws between thoughts,
as if hiccupping,
as I try to defend
my strange creativity,

and as he slips away
from my mind control and
from equal awe of our fated Canyon run-in, and
from any disappointment at the former Madi
rejecting his proposal
To the Fifth Grade Dance,

but not from my fantasy
of sweat-covered, passionate
adult things
on hilltops.

In seventh grade, Alec and I don't stare at each other anymore.

Heroine Addicts
by a [Single] High School Sweetheart

They say experience shapes you.
They say you haven't lived until you've almost died.

How is it, then, that I've hardly lived,
And I've died a thousand times?
How is it, then, that I've everything to live for,
And easy experience hasn't shaped me in the least?

I think that tragedy may live in your heart
No matter where you've been or where you're from
I think that sorrow may seep through your skin
No matter how long you've traveled or how far you've come.

They say that interest is love.
They say you can't be loved unless you're interesting.

How is it then, that I've hardly loved,
And my interest has piqued a thousand times?
How is it then, that I'm interested in love,
And no one has found me interesting in the least?

I think that passion may live in your heart
No matter who you are or who's around
I think that desire may drip out your eyes
No matter if your tears are not so profound.

They say a girl cannot have lived until she's loved.
They say they cannot love a girl who hasn't lived.

But I have neither lived, nor loved
And still, I know what longing is.
My one true depth is that I long
To experience, to dread, to die another thousand times,
If only I
Could live, and love
And be loved
Just as I am.
Just as I am not a tragic heroine,
And just as if I were.

I Think It Was the Moon

A call to the
Wide-open evening sky.
An internet line
From a line-filled guy:
And the creak of the door
Near my huge back porch
At 4 am, with a freshly shaved
thigh.

I used to sneak out of my house at night
But I think it was the Moon, all right?
I think it was the Moon.

In the green of the grass;
In the dark, turned grey;
His skeletal fingers
Engage in play.
And the longed-for kiss,
Which I knew would spark,
In the tips of his lips
Seems to fade away.

I used to sneak out of my house at night
But I think it was the Moon, all right?
I think it was the Moon.

In the stolen time
Of the deepest hours
On a haphazard blanket
We trade our powers—
The gift of my touch
To gain his respect;
The loss of my own
As his glory
sours.

He guides my hand
Under starless skies—
The soft glow from above
No eclipse for dead eyes.
The breeze on my neck
Is the needed caress,
As he moves my hand
Toward his sought-after
prize.

And the fields were just yards;
And the battles were grave;
And the humping was dry;
And I didn't need to shave;
But the dark was alive
And my body was a wolf
Who was owned by the chase
And who couldn't behave.

The douleur exquise;
The absence of sight;
The failure of desire
To yield real delight.
The disparate damning
Of romance shamed;
The race of the dark;
The embrace of my plight:

I used to sneak out of my house at night
A call from the breeze, and the blue of the light;
It surely wasn't for Mr. Right—

It was the Moon.

Punch-Drunk

The sky, is the most beautiful thing, my wine-drunk eyes, have
ever seen.
And wine makes my skin warm, and tingling
Head is high, yet thoughts are jingling,
Heart pounds lightly yet profoundly weighs
against my chest—projects my gaze
in steady patterns against the scene.

Your face, is the most beautiful thing, my tortured mind, had
ever seen.
I can't erase your magnetic force from my eyes
No matter how hard every muscle tries
Why your features appeal the most is news
to any listener who knows how you abuse
My every longing, hoping, gazing glean.

You're only an illusion,
Yet I had you for so long.
You're only selfish comfort
Yet I keep on clinging on.

Our faces shine when we're together
In that first moment, before our fate
That we promised to each other
Catches up, and proves too late.

And my drunken, tortured mind
Looks for love again, for hope
But my knowing, longing heart
Despairs to do much more than
cope.

I'll to bed before I try
to give more substance than is due
to an empty, naive vision
that was made for me by you.

And I'll fabricate your image
that I've grown to know so well
as I slink into a slumber
just to pacify this hell

With pretendings that will soothe me
With a nullifying depth
that acknowledges the feelings
Only I seem to have left.

My dreams, are the most promising thing, my twisted heart,
could ever sing.

Miss, Your Knight

I would meet you at every level
And hold your hand at every turn
Whisper softly to you when we're quiet
Only make you sizzle when you want to burn.

You may think my workings are The Devil
You may think our love would cause a riot
But I thought my touch could make you learn
That whole meals such as ours deserve no diet.

Dine with me awhile whilst we settle;
Settle not for flat wine with no bite,
Settle not, mere dust within an urn,
Don't settle down, or in, for something trite.

Mundane is just the way to make you smile.
Urbane will not assist you down the aisle.
Rage with me, and feast with me tonight
And leave your Mary Mary, Quite Contrite,

Then leave your bland remorse behind that door
And lock it up, and welcome in your Whore—
Through the window, *she* will climb—
And let our selves forget, in time
(A hasty moment)—whence we came before.

This Miss would move you every inch
Exhilarate you every hour
Never would she miss a chance
To puddle you within her power.

Share she could, as well, else lynch
The fire that made you want to dance
And never want to make lust sour
She'd sugar-surge each night's romance.

A Knight's delight is what you need!
You know a dame who'd live to feed
The ever-aching man in you
Who knows not how to own his deed.

Mary's quenched you for a while
But can she match your wicked style?
Now Maid Madeline is here—
To be your Lady, never fear—
She'll ride in on her steed and slay
Denial.

Up in Smoke

or

How You Went Back to <u>Your</u> High School Sweetheart

How we made out on my basement floor;
How we licked each other's noses and it drove us crazy;
How you pushed me up against a wall in the stairwell of your dorm
and told me you'd never felt anything like this.

How we made out, naked, in my futon bed
And without feeling you inside of me, transcended, both of us,
Into a realm of half-awareness neither one could describe
or dare to talk about afterwards.

How these moments could be false
In any way, or how they could mean less than lightning,
Confounds my sense-memory.
We were the elements igniting, joining molecules of oxygen
and nitrogen; exploding into dizziness, forgetfulness;
And perhaps—entering a haze so separate from what we're used to—
letting you block out the basement floor.

Plane One: Crashes

She went to bed without a lover:
Coke can jittering on the lonely tray,
And her laptop threatened by shaking ice;
She went to bed without a lover.

Just hours before, beneath the clouds
She said "Adieu" in glowing night,
And cast her bounds in a circle in the blue
Just hours before, beneath the clouds.

Just hours before, beneath the sun
She said goodbye to each advance,
And wrote her own name in a heart in the sand
Just hours before, beneath the sun.

And then, amongst the sun and clouds,
Her bed-side table a plastic slab
of grey against a stranger's back,
The sugary coke between her teeth,
Her stomach leapt a mile high
To join her in her joyous liberty.

She went to bed without a lover:
A childhood friend asleep by her side,
And no man threatening to keep her heart alive;
She went to sleep
alone.

Magnanimous Inanimate

If I were dead
I would roam the streets of my hometown
smiling at all the bullies I grew up with.
I would kiss them on their foreheads
and it would sting like painful love-drops—
the kind left by people whose kindness
you don't deserve. The nips would be
dewy, like moisture squeezed from a
settling mist at midnight.

But the bullies wouldn't see me there.
I would be no more present than those drops of dew.
No waving flag, no entitled declarations of what
is owed me; no curses; no hexes. Even as a
poltergeist—my powers surging uninhibited from
lack-of-body, twirling like breezes—I'd brush
right past the greasy bangs of the bullies.

Hardened souls would fold to unknown tenderness,
their heads lurching forward toward me and down
to their chests, palms joining in prayer, kneeling,
as I backed away, slipping into atmosphere.

Hair tousled, perhaps they'd crouch awhile, faces unharmed
but contorted in awe. Then clutch the freedom pouring
out of them, like *me* through drops of condensation.
I hope they'd collapse, but in liberation:
laying down their sharp inner armor and
looking up as their hell lifts like fog,
whispering a well-meaning incantation:
"Sorry. Thank you. R.I.P."

Boys in the Park

Two Boys in the Park
(a curious trope)
Charming like snakes with sibilant "sorries"—
the sorriest excuse for modern romantics.

Coiling a lone pretty girl in their pair,
Disarming the strong-willed, silent, soloist
from calling out: "Stop!"—they mean no harm,
and boys will be boys will be mischievous at times.

One is the straight man, the Other, funny—
neither is queer (though the Other admires
The One, in service of making him look
much broader—bolder—in his sullen attack.)

One may have smooth hair, the Other, wild—
He'll talk a good game but give off such goofiness
that the One's sparse comments leave lofty impressions
lingering on the earlobes of the Girl in the Park.

Since they work in tandem, it doesn't really matter
which one breaks the smile across her cheek;
her concentration, her determination
to ward off snake-like boys in the park.

She can smell a foul, but their love of
each other's brilliance—*gaming*—
is subtle like the scent of fresh flowers, not fragrance;
It does not mask anything, because it is pure.

Man's admiration of man
and of the skill in another's kill
generates a playful potion
as sweet as sunflowers.

This draft above her grin, a girl forgets
she knows how boys love to make a mess—
get covered in mud and grit, and spatter
dirt all over sunny gullibility.

Two Boys in the Park
Like playing with a lonely girl and letting her
bask in their love for one another, before
"the one" disappoints her, and makes the other
envious—but mostly, proud.

What This Like Is Love

I had not seen
such global ovals,
such gravitas in such
a cherubic face—with
ancient creases giving me
a sense of how ugly you'd be
when you're old in bed with me,

And still, those curling lips
with the freckle on top, pointed
and defined, pursed out toward mine,
and the scope of those blinking, planetary
stargazers—those would keep me lit up
without wanting to burn out of my body;
they would make me want to remain. Two players
smiling at the awesomeness of the Connect Four
from brown to turquoise, brown to turquoise,
unwavering—

Unlike our spirits: yours,
which wanted to wander away,
and mine, which wanted
to wander with you.

In *U* End? Oh!

When you tell me
You want to know my heart
I can tell you mean
You want to hold my
fleshy red valuable in your
greedy palms; and when
You call me beautiful,
I can tell you mean
I'd look like tribal jewelry
on your arm, a
pricey reminder of
what a suave and
lucky cave man you are.

But when I tell you
I want none of this,
I mean it.
I don't mean I'm scared of
the hot pulse thumping through
your wrapping wrists. It feels
just fine to be your prize, but
I know you could never
hold the orb of fire within me,
and you could never really
understand it. It would
scorch you, and it's far more
enigmatic than you even
realize. For this reason,

When I ask you to stop
believing you could
ever possess me,
it's because you can't.
You may grasp my façade,
but I am multitudes more
than the matter
you capture.

And when you
enclose my body
within your burly gate,
my heart escapes.

Sun Date

The flies
buzzed and bustled
around our forward shoulders.
You turned and smiled at me
with dusty dusk settling in, along with
the swarm of tiny, harmless insects, both
tickling our collar bones. Crash-landing on our
noses and elbows. I swatted, itched, and jumped
while you stayed coolly steadfast. Roots for feet.

Melted ice-pop orange made the sky
sticky. You pounded your second can
of beer as I slowly sipped, staring out
at the mellowing sunset through the net
of gnats. Head frontward. *Don't giggle.*
But peering at you in my periphery, the warm
irony bubbled to my cheeks in spurts: *Romance.*

We stood as long as we could.

Wicked West

Stock-Homed

You bought me golden-blue
Egyptian silk sheets, and
pillowcases to match. Helped me
pick out the pillows and same-blue
blanket, and the thick, dark blue towels
that absorb too much water but feel like
Hue Heffner bathrobes around our freshly
showered torsos. You left me your laundry bag,
also dark blue—and bought me scented candles,
and scented soaps shaped like fruit in a wicker basket. There were
bath soaps from Trader Joe's, along with $100-worth of cleansers and
real food I bought with the certificate you gave me. The back-massage
chair and the jewelry in my case—and the shaving cream you barely
used that I'm scraping clean now 'cause I ran out of mine. The hair drier
and brushes, I purchased while you visited, to have you take the head
shots that now hang on my bedroom wall, opposite which you helped
remove my window screen—lift my heavy air conditioner from one pane
to the next—and that screen in the kitchen, both that now line my walls.
Inside my closet is the climbing bag you gave me, the rope you gave me,
the t-shirts and scarf and sport clothes you gave me, the underwear and
sports bras and shaping bras you bought me, the Vicky's pajama pants
and sexy tank and everlasting Lulus that streamline my ass in the chilly
wind. The classic blue bathing suit you bought me to apologize for
ruining my others when you did my laundry, and the royal blue slutty-LA
dress you bought me from Forever 21, and the silver dress (my own) that
you loved for me to wear…The climbing shoes you helped me buy hang
from the old carabiner you gave me, while the fresh chalk blocks still
wait to be opened. In the kitchen are appliances and utensils you helped
me buy—the coffee press and tea you left (more tea bags in the
cabinet)—and the new tools that help me open dinners I cook, like the
bottle opener (mine, but that you showed me how to use). I brought the
wine you left to my party and used the giant crock pot to entertain my
guests. The potatoes you bought are still growing spuds, and I get to use
the shredder you made me get to make home fries in the morning for
another man. That wooden cutting board I knew you'd like. The gyoza
we're still eating from the freezer. And oh—you left two apple-pears in
the fridge. The living room windows were supposed to be for you to
stand in front of, naked, looking out, sipping your coffee in the daybreak

rays. You helped me pick that perfect futon, my only new piece of
furniture, that we slept on together before I bought a bed. Behind it,
tucked away, are the two yoga mats you bought—one
for you and one for me—and the yoga towel (just for
me) which, now, another man sweats on. And on it,
next to the cheap coat rack that's covered in hats
you gave me, is that little Build-a-Bear with the
heart you kissed in it, holding the baseball you
caught for me at the World Series. This home
you helped build around me so that I could
sit here and dream of you, waiting. I know you
bought me the sheets so that I'd think twice
about mucking them up with foreign fluids. But
I never did think twice. And I never asked you to.
Though
I did hesitate
I did not reject
the bedspread and clothing and cleaners and food cans and candles and
wine and appliances and futon and help, all rendered for free, but at my
body's cost. I even hoped you'd come here and fix it all up. You gave so
that I would love, but all you let me
love is what you gave. You hid behind gestures
so I couldn't see that there was nothing else.

Except your big strong arms. And your big soft heart.
And your cooking and climbing and sadness and pain. And your fight and
your drive to have someone you couldn't. And your readiness for
someone readier than me. And your delusions. Your irrational doting.
Teaching me to touch you and please you, and returning with incredible
massages and deep, caring kisses.
Through all of this force, I never rushed with such adrenaline
that your slots-for-eyes came into focus. A creamy brown, I only
caught a glimpse in there, now and again, of a real foundation. You were
sturdier than me, but you were too caught up
on the fringes and fixings. The flesh and feelings.
No mortar or cement. Then you left your trinkets, all ornaments, which
I donate now at my own discretion.

I parade around—the doll you decorated—
to attract other men to what you thought I'd be for you.
They see me in your hand-picked lingerie, they drink your wine
and I shred your potatoes for them to devour at breakfast. I cut
off the spuds so they don't seem so freshly just-several-weeks-old.
And we finish that bread I bought for you to try. We squish your bear
and drop your ball, rolling when we tumble on that futon bed. But

You were all marrow and madness
and your gifts of all sizes were heavy
clutter on my spirit. Only now that I've purged
the maker from the home, I see I am not
the wife who built it. You built me up
with things I accepted, even though
I knew it wasn't working. Like the
Bluetooth headset (thank God I
lost that), and the songs you
bought me

instead of
listening

to mine.

Dark Matters

Has the light truly escaped me,
Or am I choosing to awaken in darkness?
Perhaps I am a bat—all sonar
Sensing the world around me,
With my eyes shut, but feelings ablaze.
Writhing with input, rippling with
Assumptions that make way for
Determinations—but lost, and
Ultimately [un]guided
By my own blind clicks:
Resounding my inner
Limitations.

If my entire world is only my
Reflection, what relief can there
Be from my keen self-loathing? My own
Rejection of any other stimuli—the voice,
Or sense, of any other guide?

For some, instinct may be a savior. But in my case,
It's like the legend of the lemmings:
A broken compass stubbornly navigating
Real terrain to the edge of the Earth. As though
Ground were made of intangible parts, only airy ideas—
I am that contortion my sister saw: that beast of mental
Chatter that makes the smartest creatures
Turn on their heels once lured
By my cacophonic blizzard
Of white noise.

My call is alluring, but fastened in nighttime. It somehow
Echoes, expanding into emptiness. Flattening landscapes
Into blank slates. I am that vacuous vision. That
Sheet of bright darkness bent toward the beyond,
But lurking only in cavernous spaces. Blinding,
If you step inside—where walls of sound
Seal off my perception of
You. Myself.
A bright place to land.

Hollywoed

Your voice crackles
As you look ahead,
And I can feel inside of you
Your gentle fear of me—

As we dismantle layers of ourselves
Bullet Coffee over Hollywood.
I always said Malibu, and you, Venice—
Visions of us cutting in line,
Overcoming ethnic and internal obstacles—but here, with you,
In the limbo of the trees, with the
Mucky pool we've lounged in only once, a placid paradise,
Is home.

My own pair of pools—pale next to yours—
Shrink to slits, as I study your stories
Of other women's missteps, seeing myself in them.
Your self-opinion is high—enough to match and rise above
My own. You are committed only
To your Lone Wolf story,
And me, to my dream of being one
In a wild, Pack-Leading Pair.

But while yours tremors, my own breath—
The great modulator I consistently neglect—
Becomes steady, like with so few in my history.
A balance of power, and un-punishing energies (yours, more than mine)
Shatters platonic purpose.

Your shifty, deceiving, bottomless
Basins keep welling up without me, flowing forth
While that crackling fire in your chest
Keeps dancing the two-step, swinging me along...

And I allow myself to believe I am different:
The guise of specialness we both bolster
To gloss those shiny images of our separate selves—
Those selves that skirt the waters of anti-social media,
Fishing for (spiritual/sexual) identity. Because—unbridled—
We are both the same buzzing, amorphous, flitting force
That you call "Flow," and I still seek to harness into
"Will."

Your otherworldly ovals turn,
And lock—
And my tunnel vision reignites.
For an eternal moment, I leap into your cloudy well—
Where I've been a thousand times—
And I cannot see myself without you.
And then I remember: the Absence.
Of your will...

And I retreat, back up that murky shoot.
Back out your door. Back to my car.
Back down that Hollywood hill.
To the hard, crumbly, yellow-dusty
All-too-level ground.
To a place where you choose
Not to exist. And I

Have to forget you.

But
I carry the crackle of your voice,
The watery dance of your oval openings,
The lofty howl of your solitary dream...

I carry them through the caffeine cloud,
Through a fog of adequate conversations,
Into my one-night empty bed—
The only true stranger in my sleepless sheets.

And my insufficient slits squeeze tight, dropping
Damp residue of that alternate altitude
On the hollows beneath them (always my albatross, but
They deepen with each passing year.) You are

"Patient". I am
"Surviving"...

And I will.

Skin Deep

These waves of feeling
Were not meant for you
But for someone
Bold-hearted and tender
Nuanced and generous
Understanding and elevating—
You,
Simple and Skin-Healing,
Awkwardly swaggering (or waddling)
Oblivious to input and teetering on callous
Oddly discerning, aggressively dismissive
Even your flawless flirtation, flippant—
Your picture-pillowy lips
And chilly expression that
Curdled to be looked into:
A carving of a ritual man
Built for "hunting and gathering,"
Hoarding, meandering

And for loving me
In that one, perfect way.

Wizard of Awes

I lost my future, over and over—only,
In a blink, I was rewarded as
You whirled into every corner
of my consciousness.

Windswept—and ferocious—
Blowing constructs down
Bound by bound, frame by frame
You were loopy enough for my terrain, yet
Brave enough to admit your fear;
To see me as my loudest ego and
Quietest longing begged to believe in.

I didn't tumble into your eyes,
But you brought me there, open
And eager—sweeping me in by
My own force. In a breath, we
Met inside, along crisp but shaky
Lines, and you listened with
Heart that desired to be bold, but with
Mind not sufficiently sturdy
to hold.

A Titan Challenge

Love you and be ready to leave you
Protect my heart while it's primed to expand
Because it satisfies me (you gratify me!)—
Yet let you go the second you drop me
Decide to forget me
Reveal who you never let me be to you.

Yet, meanwhile, all the while,
Believe I might be your everything.
Let nothing faze me as we sink into doubt
Yet somehow, in the cold, keep our fire stoking—
Always burning, never out.

When I can't reach your seabed, can you have compassion?
Can I earn your empathy, but not your pity?
Can you dare to plunge my waters, many leagues deep—
Never treading, always steep—
Where submarines go and tend to implode
Where everything is too soon, yet not soon enough.

If you fell all the way in, I might stop spinning:
I'd hold on, calmly awaiting our end.
Practically peaceful (not too polite to speak)
Yet resourceful with language, economical with energy.
Clear-headed with knowing: every breath counts.
We'd share that hint of oxygen
Make doom feel more benign.

If you understood the game as I do
Would you play to win one moment more?
How fleeting it is, the Universe's hand—
We enmesh to keep warm
Our only chance to explore.
That pressure you perceive
Will be gone in a flash—
Compressing one
Or both of us
To ash.

Little Death

Staving off the thoughts—like hiccups—
Beckoning: *"Give up. Your grandiose*
Delusions of superior connection
Only flicker in and out of a hoped for
Reality."

Searing whispers gnaw at my voice box,
Claw at my esophagus—telling me: I am no good.
Not beautiful enough. Too dark.
"The problem is me," they hiss, recalling: No matter how clear the dirt
behind me of any misdeeds (like fallen leaves), of any lack of sacrifice
(devotional love), devoid of delirium or dearth (withholding); yet all this,
my side of a pebbly path through shared experience? The other
peppered with misgivings and tremors that likely
registered on the Richter scale.
Where was I to feel this rockiness? Weren't we always side-by-side?
How did I overlook my rolled heels, scraped knees,
My leading. Yet how did you still
Leave me in your dust?

Forced inside, I look out a window, imagining the girl ambitious enough
to jump—a shameful thought, immediately hand-slapped by my
pedantic inner ruler: *"You will learn to suffer instead."*

So I wonder at my own miswiring
Despite all my knowing, devotion misfiring
Undermining the gifts of my affection,
Crawling backward toward attachment, attention.
Like the made-up stillness of a glass of scotch in hand,
Across the imagined table from some "willing" man—
Take these dreams away from me!
Put me across a slab I can feel, from
The one who won't leave (not a dog at my heel).
And let traipsing through some wooded labyrinth be
A firm hand hold and eyes that can *see*
When they meet mine. In visceral time.
That won't close tight and hide. That open
All the way Alive.

What visions often cloud their minds (and
What tangible love are they all
So wary of)?

Each new sadness is a violent grief
Each hope, the shakiest promise
And each passing day, my self-
Preservation—to silence loud doubts
On the edge of fallen fancies—
A fight. For my most literal life.

Plane Two: Shut Out, Shutdown

Despair, please melt me from the skies
Crash the plane and leave my dreams
Definitively unattended. They all feel as
Hopeless as heaven on earth; I've tasted their
Teasing temptation and
I've found no respite
From my desperate undoing.
I can't build a "me" that can withstand
The daily tocking of time, waiting
For prized moments; the space between them
Endless—each one
Brutally quick.

Wall

Folds from nose to
Chin become deep
Troughs for tears,
Forged over years,
As youth and beauty
Slip quickly
Through time's fingers—
Months marked by

Grief.
Like cold columns erected
Across a sacred space,
Busted pillars prepare to keep intruders out,
Where so many have trespassed
Disguised as soulmates.

I don't think the heart was built
To withstand all the losses.
Eventually, it's bound to grow
Viny walls of stone
Cobbled together by leagues of
Disappointments.

Miles apart,
My heart and
You,
Your thoughts, your dreams—that
Blackness you saw—
I still yearn for the
Completion of
Our link. Like overlapping bricks
With an unfinished chunk
Where interlopers may pass now
Better than ever, yet no one else
May ever get
Inside.

All the while
The terms sag
Like melting mortar
Eroded by salty grimaces
Sick of holding it all
Together.

Unmasked

Your life is a masked apology
Take off! Peel the top
Of your onion skin—
Smooth and sleek, with bristly creases,
Flaking at the touch of others; rolling
Always into what is
"Right."

You're nothing if not appropriate, orderly, and therefore
Righteous. Take off the mask; each under-layer tender,
Raw and smelly, but hearty. Potent
Flesh.

And how you always hid
Beneath a veil of "strong,"
When the strength you sought
Was inside all along.

Forget Me Not

How I wish you wished to talk to me.
How I wish wooing were truly
Gender fluid
And not
An embarrassment
For the pride of
Femininity.

But this flailing derives
From a sense of
Failing.

Women take on
The life of a man
And then, men misplace them
Interchangeable like socks, but

Forget me!
I want no more skin in that game:
How well I treated you and
Whether you even
Noticed.

Forget me!
How I burnt holes
In our skulls
As I coiled around you
A charge from roots to God.

My game was in *your* image:
Your eyes, your hair, your hands
In your service and asking only
To go deeper into the wild
Unknown, building
Amorphous monuments
To living fully
Together.

Women are taught
That we can forget you
As long as we're sure that
You'll never forget *us*.

With the help of the heavens
I'm giving this up.

Forget me! How,
When you leaned in,
You opened. Trusting
In my words of wisdom and
In the chance there might be
Nothing better
Out there.

I won't forget
How much I supported
How little I demanded
How much I devoted.
My martyrdom does nothing
For my sanity, but
It reminds me how precious is
The resource of
My energy.

I won't forget you: that's not
How I'm wired. But you
Can go ahead. My ghost
Won't need to haunt you and
The next girl won't need to know
Your pattern is established. I won't
Check in, I won't send gifts. I won't
Think of all the birthdays

I know you'll
Forget.

Eventually.

I'll forget to care that

You don't.

Fallen

Love is just not like they said in the movies
So many women, aging, hardened
Skin toughening as it loosens, hearts hard like stolen safes
You can see the envy in their eyes; jealous of stories
Tried and told; lovers lost painfully, discarded from memory
Protectively. With only echoes of the faint scent of
Deceit.

These women want to open like buds,
But they've been told, time and again, that
Their journey is over. If they didn't meet
Prince Charming when they were 14, or 25
They're no longer broken in the ticklish way—
No young woman will envy their jaded knowing: that
No young man will sweep in and break them down.

The boys who *might* embrace a momentary challenge,
Tethered not to even their own longings for longevity.
How fun to tease and taunt dried flowers—
Warm them with mist, see petals enliven as
Enriching color seeps down, deep as soil—
Only to prune up again when sweet water wanders,
Draining out.

Wry

If your hands could knead me like dough
Work out my kinks
Roll me flat
And pat me back together again,
Ready to be baked and bred and reborn,
I would rise to the occasion:
I would not contest.

Lesion

I'm not sure that time heals all wounds
Some fester, interminably,
Some scar in a jarring way
Haunting our eyeballs every day
A reminder of what's never coming soon.

Loss is a sore that scabs
And even when it flakes away
It leaves a mark—some light, some dark—
That without ignoring, always seems to stay.

This incorporation—like permanently squinting—
Is the only course toward pain's erasure. Forgetting
With deliberation, falls short of bloodletting—or
Lobotomy (the only true cure for wounds this
Pure), decidedly out of reach.

Deep cuts are often
Self-inflicted
By the mind. And, in time
We can learn how to make
Few new ones. To let other humans
Only leave scratches or stretches.
To look back fondly on those
Lumps and bruises, we must acknowledge
We've been decrepit travelers, no better or
Worse than those who hurt us.

Can we find the magic
Of smooth skin grown over
Those thrashes and gashes
Of our past? This must be
Sheer alchemy, and underneath
I do not believe we lose the sheath—
Hard tissue forms the lesson around
The lesion; that freckle is the splinter
In your palm you never had the tools
Or proper patience to remove. And yes,
Some others may, one day, find it beautiful.
If we can choose the friends with less friction
On the road toward sunrise that embraces our
Midnights. The people who don't blame us
For losing baboonish battles, for getting
Roughed up, for our blemishes. Those people
Will persist, as do our ghosts and our gashes—
As we do.

Drama-tique

Yes, I want my movie ending
But I don't want no movie scene.
I want that Happy Ever After,
Not the drama in between.

I want fireworks and laughter
Tears of joy and lightning bugs
I don't want the death and torment
Sex and roll and rock and drugs—

Those are my means to an end.
Those are the things that abuse.
Those are the fluff in the middle.
They *aren't* the stuff that I choose:

I yearn for…
I breathe for…
I hope for…
I wait for…

The End.

ABOUT THE AUTHOR

Her laugh may scare you. She's more mind than body—but she tries to live where the universe placed her.

Madeline Blue is an actor and writer of poetry, songs, screenplays, and other people's memoirs. She received her BA in Evolution and Behavior from Tufts University (with Highest Honors for her thesis on "The Biology of Bias"—pretentious, no?) For over 15 years of collaboration, she has brought visions to life through script consulting, pitch and proposal development, content editing, and ghostwriting for entrepreneurs and artists. Her forte is hyper-realistic stories with heady leads who battle their own humanity.

Where sadness meets absurdity, she finds authenticity. She likes to share gently dark, deeply personal stories in an attempt to normalize the pain of existing.

Shared loneliness is freedom.

Find Madeline's poetry and songs in progress @littleladyditties on Instagram
and a portfolio of her other written works at
www.madeline.blue.